T0012146

DONKEY KONG:

PROTECTOR OF DK ISLAND

x1981

Kenny Abdo

Fly!
An Imprint of Abdo Zoom
abdobooks.com

abdobooks.com

Published by Abdo Zoom, a division of ABDO, P.O. Box 398166, Minneapolis, Minnesota 55439. Copyright © 2022 by Abdo Consulting Group, Inc. International copyrights reserved in all countries. No part of this book may be reproduced in any form without written permission from the publisher. Fly!™ is a trademark and logo of Abdo Zoom.

Printed in the United States of America, North Mankato, Minnesota.
102021
012022

Photo Credits: Alamy, Everett Collection, Getty Images, iStock, Pond5, Shutterstock, ©SobControllers p.4, 6 / CC BY 2.0, ©Farley Santos p.16 / CC BY-SA 2.0, ©Mariofan13 p.20 / CC BY-SA 4.0
Production Contributors: Kenny Abdo, Jennie Forsberg, Grace Hansen
Design Contributors: Candice Keimig, Neil Klinepier

Library of Congress Control Number: 2021940182

Publisher's Cataloging-in-Publication Data

Names: Abdo, Kenny, author.
Title: Donkey Kong: protector of DK Island / by Kenny Abdo
Other Title: protector of DK Island
Description: Minneapolis, Minnesota : Abdo Zoom, 2022 | Series: Video game heroes | Includes online resources and index.
Identifiers: ISBN 9781098226930 (lib. bdg.) | ISBN 9781644947388 (pbk.) | ISBN 9781098227777 (ebook) | ISBN 9781098228194 (Read-to-Me ebook)
Subjects: LCSH: Video game characters--Juvenile literature. | Donkey Kong (Game)- Juvenile literature. | Nintendo video games--Juvenile literature. | Heroes--Juvenile literature.
Classification: DDC 794.8--dc23

TABLE OF CONTENTS

DONKEY KONG

Peeling away his bad-guy image, Donkey Kong is a video game hero fans go bananas for.

Throughout the decades, DK and his family have become some of the most **iconic mascots** for Nintendo.

PLAYER PROFILE

Creator Shigeru Miyamoto wanted to base a game around a man, his girlfriend, and the man's pet ape that turns against him.

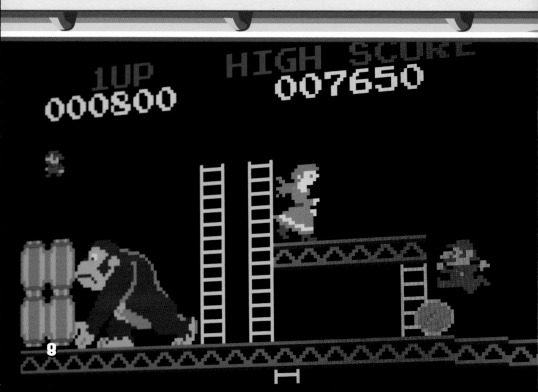

1UP   HIGH SCORE
000800   007650

Miyamoto was influenced by the movie *King Kong* and the story *Beauty and the Beast*. For the ape's name, he chose "Donkey" because it is a headstrong animal.

The game was called *Donkey Kong*.
It came out in 1981 and was a huge
success. Four **sequels** quickly followed!
The **titular character** was now too big
to share the screen.

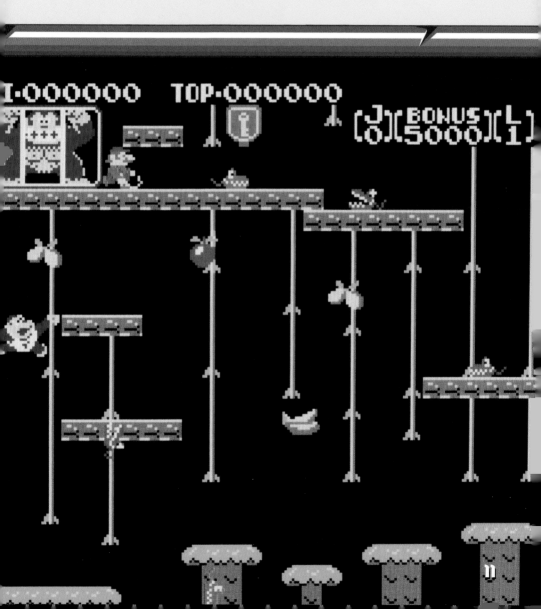

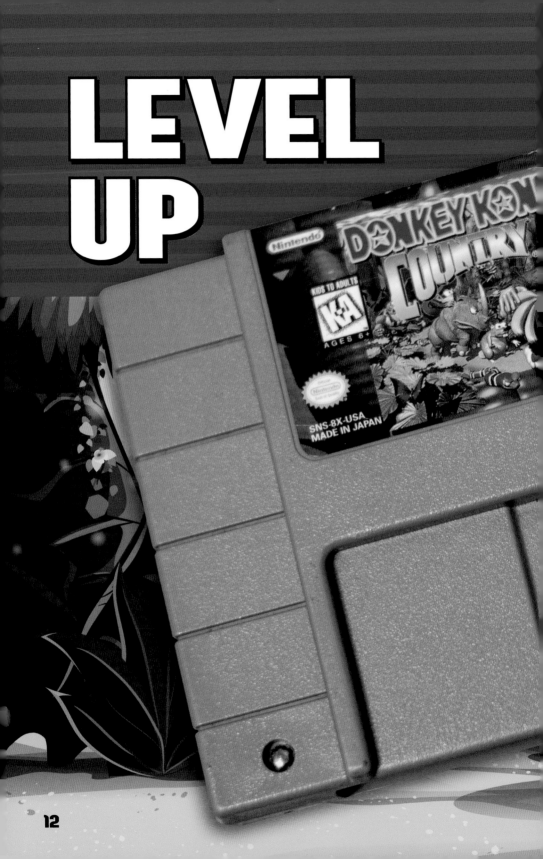

LEVEL UP

Donkey Kong Country smashed all expectations in 1994. Giving DK his own island, fans could now control him as a hero! Their love for DK made it the fastest-selling video game at the time!

The next two **sequels** introduced more of DK's family. Players got to meet and control Dixie, Diddy, and Wrinkly Kong who all quickly became fan favorites.

DONKEY KONG 64

PRESS START

©1999 NINTENDO. GAME BY RARE.

In 1999, *Donkey Kong 64* changed everything with 3D gameplay! For the next decade, DK would go on to do many rhythm and racing **spin-offs**. He returned to his island in 2010 for *Donkey Kong Country Returns*!

Tropical Freeze followed in 2014. EDP Tokyo released a new DK adventure in 2021 to celebrate the game's 40th anniversary!

DK steals the show in many other games. He is featured in every *Mario Kart* and *Super Smash Bros.* game. DK also popped up in many *Mario Party* and *Mario* sports games throughout the years.

EXPANSION PACK

DK swung from video games to the big and small screen, too! He was featured in many Saturday morning cartoons, as well as 40 episodes of his own show.

Guinness World Records honored the series with seven awards! The records included "First Use of Visual Storytelling in a Video Game," for the original **arcade** version.

DK and his adventures have sold more than 40 million copies worldwide, making him a barrel of fun for everyone.

GLOSSARY

arcade – a coin-operated entertainment machine often installed in public spaces.

iconic – commonly known for its excellence.

mascot – a person or thing that is used as a symbol for a particular event or company.

sequel – a video game that continues the story begun in a preceding one.

spin-off – a certain story or game that comes from a larger story.

titular character – character in a book, film, video game, etc. from whom the name of the work takes its title.

ONLINE RESOURCES

Booklinks
NONFICTION NETWORK
FREE! ONLINE NONFICTION RESOURCES

To learn more about Donkey Kong, please visit abdobooklinks.com or scan this QR code. These links are routinely monitored and updated to provide the most current information available.

INDEX